Lean Analytics

How to Use Data to Track, Optimize, Improve and Accelerate Your Startup Business

Table of Contents

Introduction

I wrote this book basing from words of experts, online influencers, and personal opinions.

Many people already wrote books about this topic. Why still write one if that's the case? That's because of the explosion of information about this topic. It made it inevitable for people to generate different and new interpretations. Their words can confuse individuals who want to learn about it.

Unlike those books written before this, this book aims to serve as a short guide. Treat it as a supplementary source of information if you will. It will not pander on claiming that this is the one single book you need to master the subject.

Many people have already jumped on the bandwagon. They created websites with domain names using the words lean, startup, and analytics. Visit them and all they want is to get something from you instead of them giving anything worthwhile. It's easy for people to get misinformed when they research because of those sites. Not to mention that the web isn't exactly moderated and curated for its accuracy.

Aside from that, there are other factors that complicate things:

1. Experience and application of the theory resulted into a different realization
2. Different backgrounds of people influence a different opinion
3. Excessive recycling of facts and opinions passed from one person to the next

The goal of this book is to give its readers a primer about lean analytics. I'd be honest here: it's not actually complex. It will only become complex if you put it in action and you have already a lot of data to analyze.

Since that's out of the way, here's a short story I want to tell you.

As you might have already guessed, I'm an entrepreneur. My first business flopped. I wasted my savings and the money I loaned. And I learned little from my experience after the business fell.

Let me tell the optimistic people that the failure wasn't worth it. It's like learning that a wooden bridge will collapse if you walk on it by walking on it. You could have saved yourself by asking the guy living near the bridge if it's stable enough.

A failed first business is like that. You are going to enter an unfamiliar territory. The first thing you should do is to ask the people who are already in that place. It should've been common sense.

People should stop preaching that it's normal to fail on your first attempt. It's plain wrong. If you believe that, you're actually setting yourself into an expensive failure.

What I did after the blunder was to cool myself down for a while. I took some jobs to pay the loan. Some of those loans came from friends and relatives. Of course, I also needed to have money for the usual daily expenses and the dreadful monthly bills. It's a painful and shameful experience.

I cleared all the baggage that came with the failed startup. I decided that it was time to look back on what happened. I wanted to know if it's still possible for me to be the businessman I aspired to be.

As I found out, I was wrong with everything. That wounded my ego. But I suppressed it believing it's already too late for me to whine about something that's passed. There's no use crying over spilled milk, especially if it's already dried and spoiled.

Going back to my postmortem, there were two primary things that attributed to my failure.

1. I failed to perform intensive research. I thought the knowledge of relatives and friends was enough. I asked the ones who have established businesses. I was wrong.

   But it doesn't mean that what they taught me was wrong. They don't work anymore. I could have succeeded if I started my business two decades ago. But the entrepreneurship landscape has changed a lot in the past few years.

   Let me use my previous analogy. They were miles away from the bridge I was going to cross. I asked them if I can cross the bridge that appears to be already collapsing. They said yes, having no idea about what I was talking about. That was dumb of me.

2. I relied on instinct. I was confident. I thought I can delve into the mind of my customers. I thought that I can predict their behavior. I was, again, dead wrong. And it was my fatal mistake.

It was stupid of me. Why do I need to do that in the first place? I should have asked the customers themselves. Why try to emulate them if they're already there waiting for me to ask them.

Of course, I wasn't able to think of those things right off the bat. I was able to get some help. And the help I got was in the form of a book, The Lean Startup, written by Eric Reis.

But before I delve into that, I want you to know that both Lean Startup and Analytics helped me with my new venture. It's not that my business became one of the Fortune 500, but running it feels different and much better.

During my first venture, I was always lacking sleep. I always pushed myself harder every day thinking about all the things going on with the business. And despite the effort and sacrifices, nothing worked out.

I was borderline depressed after the catastrophe, which was my first business. But now, I didn't have to do too much. Well, I still do more since I'm running lean. I don't have full time employees, instead I have a few freelancers.

But I don't have to think too much. Instead of scrambling my brain on how I can improve my business, I can ask my customers. They are more than willing to tell me what I need to do and what they want. I do what they say, and I can sustain them and make them loyal.

I don't have to dizzy up myself with numbers, trying to measure if I am doing the right things or not. Currently, my Only Metric That Matters is sales count. If I have more sales, I'm doing better. If there's few then that's the time I need to put in more effort.

There are no guessing games anymore or prioritization. My business expenses are also a lot lower now. I don't rent an office or warehouse anymore. Everything's done at home. When it comes to logistics and other services, I hire the right businesses and people that can do the task I need to do.

I guess that's enough stories for now.

What I can promise you is this. Doing lean startup and lean analytics can make your mind rest easy. It's not the surefire success method, I admit that. Because if it is, I won't even bother to write this book. I would instead enjoy my vacations and earned money.

I can't say that it's a surefire method to prevent your business from failing. But I can promise that it will reduce the risk of losing your business.

Sure, some say that the amount of success is relative to the risk you are willing to take. I take that as truth. I would rather be a semi-successful businessman if it means I can keep my sanity. I wouldn't want to live a life filled with anxiety thinking how I can repay my loans when my business fails.

For those who want to start a business. I recommend running lean. It doesn't matter if you're a layman who wants to turn his life around and be the boss or if you're a business graduate. Running lean is the best way to start a business today.

With that said, the book contains information on how you can exactly do that. I would like to repeat that this book is a result of research and experience. But I promise you that after you finish this book, you'll have a different perspective as an entrepreneur who wants to establish a startup business.

Chapter 1

Lean Startup and Analytics The Discussion You've Been Waiting For

"Lean Startup isn't about being cheap [but is about] being less wasteful and still doing things that are big."

— Eric Reis

This chapter's goal is to let you understand the basics of Lean Startup and Analytics. It will talk about their definitions and how they work, and why they have been developed. Also, it will teach you on how to have a data driven mindset. Having a data-driven mindset will make it easier for you to apply lean analytics in your business.

What Is Lean analytics?

Benjamin Yoskovitz is one of the authors behind the Lean analytics book. According to him, lean analytics is an approach to improve your business. It relies on you focusing on one single metric to measure your progress toward your goals. The book refers to that metric as the One Metric That Matters. It's pretty straightforward, don't you think?

To start with Lean analytics, you should have great knowledge of the industry you're in. You should also know the current state of your business. Is it on its way to success? Is it failing? Or everything is doing fine with no signs of sudden success or failure?

The next step is to set a goal. It can be better sales or it can be company expansion. Once the goal is set, you will need to determine your One Metric That Matters. If your goal is better sales, your One Metric That Matters is the number of sales your company will make.

Lean analytics isn't a static approach—it was before. Every business has its own unique needs and it changes, depending on the state it is in. This means that you need to change your One Metric That Matters from time to time. You need to reevaluate your company's performance and goal to know the proper metric to use next time.

Startups and Lean analytics

Lean analytics restrains a business from losing its focus on its goal. Startups benefit from it. It helps them overcome the initial pitfalls of starting a business. That pitfall is the fervor to do all things at once and recover investments made.

Lean analytics pushes startups away from going through premature scaling or growth. Instead of expanding, it pushes a business to establish a solid foundation. Businesses using lean analytics become solutions specialists.

It gives the company a direction, and a very narrow one at that. As mentioned before, lean analytics uses a single metric to measure progress. This approach has been developed from a business methodology called Lean Startup.

Lean Startup

Lean startup is a business methodology that promotes running a business as lean as it can. Steve Blank and Eric Reis helped popularize it.

The methodology encourages an entrepreneur to start a business with minimal resources. This includes minimizing employees, products, and services.

Regular and large-scale businesses use a Swiss knife to operate. A lean startup only uses a sharp and flexible single knife.

As the business operates, it improves and adds elements to the business when needed. Progression means the business obtains essential tools to help the single knife.

Build, Measure, and Learn

When it comes to product and service development, a Lean Startup uses lean analytics. Lean analytics follows a simple build, measure, and learn development cycle.

For example, if the entrepreneur has an idea for a product, he'll start to build. He'll then measure and test the product. He'll then gather data from the measurements. And then he'll learn how he can improve the product based on data and lean analysis.

The improvements learned are ideas that he'll use to build again. The cycle repeats until he creates the perfect product.

During the measurement and learn cycles, companies undergo five stages:

1. Empathy: Connecting to customers and knowing what they want.
2. Familiarity: Making your brand, products, and services stick to customers' minds.
3. Virality: Making non-customers discover your brand, product, or service.
4. Revenue: Developing methods to further improve revenue from your products and services.
5. Scale: Enlarging your reach and customer base.

For example, you have built a new car model. You will first deal with the customers and test the product. Once they finish testing the car, you will gather data from them by asking for feedback. You then enter the learn and build phase again.

In the next measurement phase, you will then make your way to introduce the car to more people. You'll do that by making the car more appealing. Then another cycle goes by.

After that, you will focus on the revenue aspect of the new car. If you learn that the model is viable for your business, then you can start scaling your production.

To move through the stages, you need to follow the hook model. The hook model has four phases. They are:

1. Trigger: Event that needs to be done to start the lean analytical stage.
2. Action: Action that needs to be done to act upon the trigger.
3. Variable Reward: Motivator to make the action continue.
4. Investment: Motivator to make the stakeholders proceed to the next stage.

The Pitfall

Amateurs, like me before, always tend to get trapped in the wrong mindset. When they start a business, they tend to think that it's as simple as:

1. Think of a product

2. Develop the product
3. Sell the product
4. Profit!

Mind you, that's not a bad mindset to have. After all, you can simplify a business like that. The only problem is that they get stuck with that simplification. They fail to see or discover the intricacies behind every process.

For example, an entrepreneur wants to start a coffee shop. He finds a location for it. Build the shop. List the menu he wants to be present on the shop. And opens it. And like before, his business fails. Why did that happen?

The problem is that the coffee shop owner thought that he's done after the initial stage. He thought that the business will grow by itself.

Unfortunately, you can't plant a seed, water it for a few days, let it grow by itself, and harvest the fruit after. You can't treat a business that way. You don't stop and wait.

For one, you should never end the connection between you and the customer after he buys your product. Your job isn't done yet if someone gets your service and product. You should get feedback.

Customer feedback is the most important element in a successful business. The wants of the customer are your ticket to success.

For example, do you still remember Twilight? Do you remember the time when it was the most popular romance book title on the market? Because of its immense popularity, many amateur and veteran authors had an idea. They took it to themselves to write books about vampires.

What happened? Did another vampire story become popular? No. What happened was that Fifty Shades of Gray took the throne. Was that a vampire story? No. So why did it become popular?

The author of that book is a fan of Twilight's author. And she knows well what made Twilight good. She was a customer. It wasn't about the vampires. It was about the kind of romance that made the book sell well.

It's the same for other products. Just because bubble tea is popular doesn't mean that people will buy bubble tea from you. Customers have individual needs. And if you want your product to sell, your product must meet those needs. If a certain bubble tea is popular, get one and analyze it. Talk to the people who drink that product, and ask what they like.

Use the feedback and imitate the tea. Sell it. And you now have a higher chance of having a successful business.

Lean Startup: Your Business Doesn't Matter, Your Customer Does

The core concept in lean startup is communication to customers. It's the crucial element that shouldn't be ignored.

Entrepreneurs should create and develop businesses because of love of people. That sounds cheesy and cringe worthy. But businesses should be built to serve first; make their owners profit second.

Businesses are solutions providers and product suppliers. Products and services must fix a problem and please the desire of customers. A business' existence and its success depend on the needs and wants of people.

If you already have a lean startup running, it's never too late to shift your focus to your customers. You can start by doing these four steps:

1. Customer Discovery. Test ideas on what the customer needs, interest on the product, and business viability.

2. Customer Validation. Test the viability of the business through product sales. A product sales road map is generated. If the road map is doable and repeatable, the business is viable.

3. Customer Creation. Business plans are executed to expand and scale customer acquisition. Create customer demands to direct and improve sales.

4. Company Building. The last process. The transition from being a lean startup to a real business. It focuses on completing the business. Employees, products, and functionalities that it needed before are added.

Supply and Demand

A business is there to complete the equation of supply and demand. Most entrepreneurs nowadays either don't know that or are focused on other things. This is especially true about new entrepreneurs who're running their first startups.

It is somewhat understandable. You'll feel that you need to focus on how you can get your money back fast. The feeling intensifies if you have limited or loaned money. Believe me. I was in that situation, too.

Unfortunately, it's difficult to shift your attention to anything else. You are pressured. You must achieve results. There's no time to waste. You'll jilt the existence of your role to meet the demands of your customers. This then leads to your imminent failure.

In lean startups, you need to treat your businesses as an experiment. This experiment aims to answer two core questions.

1. Do people need this product?
2. Can I build a business around it?

You don't create a product and push it to people. It's true that if there's no need for a product, you should create one. It's a sound approach, but why would you try to do that if you can pick a product that there's already a need for? Again, supply and demand.

If your answer to the first question is yes, then you should deal with the second. Answering that question will lead to tons more. Here are a few of the follow up questions:

1. Is the product you have profitable?
2. Is there demand for your product?
3. If it isn't, can you make it so?
4. What are the steps you need to do to get that?
5. Can you even compete with the other businesses offering the same product?

In your quest to find answers to those questions, you need to use Lean analytics and have a data driven mindset to do so. And that's going to be discussed in the next chapter.

Takeaway

Lean startup is a methodology in running a business. It encourages entrepreneurs to have a bare-bones startup. It makes business owners focus on two things: customers and products.

Lean analytics is an approach developed with lean startup in mind. It encourages data analysis and logic to measure and act upon a business' progress. This leads to the introduction of the one metric that matters.

The one metric that matters is a chosen metric that's used as a measurement tool. Its purpose is to track the progress of the business towards the owner's goal.

Lean analytics also empowers lean startup's product development cycle. The cycle involves three stages: build, measure, and learn.

- The build phase takes an idea and turn it into an actual product.
- The measure phase tests the products to get useful data.

- The lean phase uses data gathered to improve the product or gain insight on what's the next business step.

You must be focused on customers and be data driven. You need to be like that to harness the effectiveness of both the methodology and approach. Both will be discussed in the next chapter.

Chapter 2

Your Journey to Become a Data Driven Person

"The price of light is less than the cost of darkness."

—Arthur C. Nielsen

For you to take full advantage of Lean analytics, you should become a data driven person. You should value the importance of every snippet of data you can gather. And give utmost care when processing them a logical manner.

Two things that you should remember when approaching matters in a data driven manner:

- Never ignore existing data, and never prioritize new data over old data.
- Squeeze out huge amounts of data as possible.
- Make data presentable and understandable
- Legally and ethically get data

- Data should back your every decision

A data driven mindset can also help you:

1. Learn industry knowledge. The industry has its own methods, techniques, skills, and tactics. They were developed to make things fruitful and easier for entrepreneurs. They didn't appear out of nowhere. They were developed, thanks to the continuous work to gather and process data. If you were able to do the same, you'll have one that you can call your own.

2. See all the opportunities. Have an eye out for every small thing happening in your business. It'll allow you to have greater insight and idea on what to do next if a problem arises. You'll also see every opportunity that you can take advantage of.

3. Understand your competitors. Things happen for a reason. If your competitors are having the upper hand or failing hard, you'll know the reason why using analytics. It allows you to imitate best practices and avoid game losing actions.

4. Have full grasp of lean analytics. Lean analytics is useless if you don't value data

and think logically. And it isn't restricted to analytics alone. A data driven mindset can help you create logical and proper business decisions. This is true regardless if you have a lean startup or not.

Remember that lean analytics seeks to remove any wasteful actions and decisions. It promotes valuable actions during the early stages of your company or startup. And with those benefits, it will effectively raise your chances of success.

Now, it's time to get more intimate with Lean analytics. At this point, the previous chapter has already given you many pointers. Those hints on how to apply lean analytics on your business or startup are there to get got your feet wet. This chapter will provide you with a chance to do some deep diving.

The One Metric That Matters

Later in this chapter, you will learn about data collection, relation, and types. If you can, it's a good time to decide the one metric that matters for you.

To make it easy for you to know that metric, follow the simple steps below.

The Customers

The first and crucial step is to get acquainted to your customers and extract data from them. There are many ways to do this, and the step you need to do depends on how you do business.

Up Close and Personal

The subtitle says it all. Just talk to them. You don't need to interrogate them or shower them with questions. You don't need to think of leading questions. Build rapport and connect to them.

Build a connection with them, and data gathering will be easier. Do that, and they'll comfortably give you feedback and other information you need. Plus, they will appreciate the effort and time you give to them.

Of course, this is highly effective on startups. And the ones that rely on foot traffic and walk-in customers will benefit from this strategy.

Customer Service

Customer service representatives get the most interaction with customers. Actually, whoever's on phone duty will have the most interaction.

You can get friendly and establish rapport on the phone like with the previous method. But unlike personal conversations, phone calls often end short.

Be sure to take the opportunity to ask for feedback at the end of each call. Be polite and don't push the customer too much for information.

Customer Feedback Form

A customer feedback form will be impersonal, regardless of how you word it. It'll never be considered warm and friendly for customers. It's a cold way to gather feedback and it's often considered a bother.

Also, customers who actually fill up feedback forms often have negative things to say. Consumers have the tendency to not bother themselves with surveys. This is especially true if they're okay with the product or service they received.

If they are pissed, you'll likely hear from them. As long as they're given the chance to talk, they definitely let you know what's on their minds. This makes customer feedback forms a good way to fish out negative impressions.

Observe Your Business Processes

Making your business lean is like taking all the fat out of a cut of meat. But unlike meat, not all fat in your business can be seen easily by the naked eye. Because of that, you need to devote some of your time to observe the processes happening in your business.

The things you can find and remove from your business can vary. Some of those are:

1. Employees who slack off too much
2. Inefficient work processes
3. Unnecessary business expenses
4. Unproductive overtimes
5. Wasteful usage of electricity, Internet, water, etcetera

Removal of the Unneeded Elements

The next step after finding the inefficiencies in your business is to remove them all.

Check the Changes in Your Metric

After doing all the previous steps, check if there is some improvement in your metric. If there is, it means that you have done something right and the metric is spot on. If there isn't, the metric isn't a good indicator, and you should come up with another one.

Oiling the System

Removing people and inefficiencies have one inevitable result: change. People hate change. In case you still have employees, be sure to reward them for their good work. Assure them that they are essential.

Introduce Improvements

Once your business is working at its best state, it's time to introduce some improvements. This part of the process is entirely up to you.

You can try to imitate some of the processes your competitors do. You can check out some books about businesses to learn more on how you can improve your operations.

Of course, you can focus on the One Metric That Matters, and check the data you gathered to get an idea on what to do next.

The Data for Your Analytics

Analytics is a measure of progress towards one's goals. You need to learn your goals first before you can consider a metric. It's been iterated before, but here are some extra things that you should learn.

The first and most important step in creating a good metric is to gather good amounts of proper data. The data should pass certain qualities and requirements. And those qualities and requirements are:

Comparable

A single point of data only gives little information. For example, selling three products today provides little and useful information. It can't help you measure your progress alone.

It gives you a starting point. Yet it needs another point of data for it to be actually useful in measuring your progress.

Say that you sold three products today and sold nine products yesterday. You can generate much more measurable information from that situation.

You can synthesize the two data points and evaluate it. You can learn that your product performed poorly today compared to yesterday. Collect comparable data points to measure your progress.

Understandable

If you don't understand a data point, it becomes irrelevant. For example, if you live in the UK, you'll be much more familiar with kilometers rather than miles.

Ask an American how far a place is from where you're standing. Expect that he will give you a distance value using the Imperial miles.

The answer you'll get is correct and true. But, it becomes irrelevant because you might have no idea how far a mile is.

Because of that, you should know how to process data to make it understandable and relevant. Here's a quote often attributed to Einstein, "It should be possible to explain the laws of physics to a barmaid."

Actually, Ernest Rutherford said that. Anyway, if it's possible, then you can understand and explain the data you got.

Rate-able

A data point is convertible or translatable to numbers. It should be always in the form of a ratio or percentage. After all, you can always process raw data or numbers to ratio or percentage.

For example, you sold three phones yesterday and nine phones today. It's easier and informational if you interpret the data by using ratio or percentage.

You can say, there is a 300% increase of phone sales in your retail store today.

But of course, play safe with this one. As William Bruce Cameron said it best in his book Informal Sociology: A Casual Introduction to Sociological Thinking, "Not everything that can be counted counts, and not everything that counts can be counted."

Relevant

As mentioned before, the metric or data must be relevant. A relevant metric can make you think of improvements and changes. An irrelevant metric is something good to know.

A customer bought three things from your company today. Sure, you can understand what it means. But does it tell you anything? Is it relevant? What did the customer buy? It's true that it is understandable. The data is simple: customers bought three things from you.

It becomes irrelevant because it doesn't provide any context. It doesn't have any accompanying information to make it relevant as a metric. When gathering understandable data, it's much better to have your data points to be specific and detailed.

For example, the customer bought three iPhone units from your retail store today. The context changes and you understand the relevance of the information. You can evaluate that your iPhone units are getting more popular than other phones in your store.

Remember that it's much better to have more data and discard the excess. Having less data only restricts you to what you can learn.

Eight Types of Data

This is where it gets interesting. You should know that there are at least eight types of data. You can use those to create a business metric to measure your business' progress. Most lean analytics use the first two types for the one metric that matters.

But it should help you out if you know the eight data types to prevent you from improperly using them. Other types aside from qualitative and quantitative can help you create unique metrics. Those metrics might not help you measure progress, but can help you in other things such as marketing, company management, and the likes.

Qualitative

This includes customer interviews or anything that doesn't involve numbers. It can be in the form of gut feeling or personal feedback. This gives you insights. This allows you to think on how you can gather or collect data for the next type of metric.

Qualitative data is often converted to quantitative. For example, feedback can be converted into numbers: 5 for positive, 0 for negative. A product's success can be measured this way.

However, data in its qualitative form is useful in lean analytics. The comments from customers can help in the development cycle of your products.

Quantitative

This is mostly numbers. It's the most used type of data that businesses use regardless if they're running lean or not. The data you get from this type of metric allows you to know the data you actually need to gather.

Unlike qualitative, you can't easily revert quantitative data to qualitative. What you can do is to interpret it. Data can be reformed or skewed through interpretation.

Vanity

It only makes you feel good. It does not help you create actionable plans that matter for your company. And it's often wrongly used as a metric to measure progress. It still serves as a good motivator and marketing material for businesses.

Actionable

Actionable often comes internally from your organization. But it can be gathered from customer feedback, too. Actionable data and metrics can provide you with insights. These insights can directly affect and influence your business decisions.

Exploratory

This is speculative data, one that's generated using currently available data on hand. This can involve predictions on how metrics will change over time. It can also show how the metrics can be influenced to achieve the result you want.

Reports

Data gathered from reports can be actionable, vanity, exploratory, or lagging. It can be generated internally or you can source it from third parties. It is often acquired by businesses periodically, depending on how you set it.

Lagging

People usually call lagging data as historical data. Not all data can be acquired instantly. Some of your business actions require some time to see results. This results can be interpreted as usable data.

Leading

The biggest difference between leading and exploratory data is the time range it predicts. Exploratory data are often predictions set to the far future. Leading is predicted for data in the near future.

Data Linking: Causality and Correlation

Data are often related or linked in one way or another. Two types of data relationship are causal and correlational.

1. Correlational: Two data points behave in a similar way because of another data point. For example, the number of umbrella sales goes up and the number of people getting flu goes up, too. You know that people buying umbrellas do not actually increase people getting sick. But you can say that it's the rainy season, which can cause umbrella sales go up and flu victims go up.

2. Causal: Two data points behave in a similar way because one of the two causes the other to change. The two data points can be considered independent or dependent. For example, it's rainy and it causes people to get sick. The

independent data is the rainy weather. And the dependent data is people getting sick. People getting sick does not cause rainy weather, but rainy weather can cause people to get sick.

What does data relationships have to do with Lean Analytics?

1. Correlational data can help you predict events. For example, next month is the start of the rainy season. You can predict that the number of people buying umbrellas and getting sick will skyrocket.
2. Causal data can help you affect the future. If you sell umbrellas before the rainy season starts, you can help prevent people from getting sick.

Data Link Testing

Unfortunately, the relationship between data is not always obvious. You can just say that two data points are causal or correctional.

To know the relationship between your data, you must perform these processes.

1. Find correlation
2. Test causality
3. Optimize causal factor

You now have a full grasp of lean startup and analytics. You are also more data driven than ever. The next step is to learn more about the technical side of things. We're going to talk about Minimum Viable Product. And we will apply what you have learned so far using examples.

Takeaway

Lean startup and analytics won't work without a data-driven mindset. Lean analytics is a research focus method of running a business. Without data, it's useless.

Don't rely on passive experience and mistakes. Focus on actively learning all the things you can with lean startup and analysis.

Of course, an unguided research doesn't bring anything to the table. You need to be precise with the information you gather. Because of that, you need to handpick the data you get to make your analyses fruitful for your company.

The center of it all is the one metric that matters. It's the single data point that will guide and tell you about the progress of your company. The only challenge is that you need to know what that metric will be.

The first thing you should do when you start operating is to realize what your company's goal is. The metric you choose should be directly tied to your goal. It should be also capable of measuring your progress.

To make your business lean and efficient, you need to work on the following:

First, have a metric that's actually useful. You should know how to figure it out, and where and how to get the necessary data for it. The best source is your customers. That is why lean analytics pushed you to be customer and product centric.

There are three common ways on how you can get your data from them. They are: up and personal, customer service, and customer feedback form.

The next steps are to observe your business processes. After that, remove unneeded elements from it and check the changes in your metric. If the metric says you progressed, proceed on oiling your system. Lastly, introduce improvements and repeat everything.

The data you gather will flood you as your business operates. Ideally, getting all the data you can get will be excellent for your analytics.

Since you're running lean, you might be the only person working on the data. It's okay be a bit selective on the data you harvest.

There are four characteristics that your data must have. They must be comparable, understandable, rate-able, and relevant. Without those qualities, you're wasting your time collecting data.

Some of those useless data can be converted into something useful. But you wouldn't want to spend the little amount of time you have, considering that you have a lot of things to do.

And then there's also the eight types of data. You have qualitative, quantitative, vanity, actionable, exploratory, reports, lagging, and leading. Be sure to choose the right of data for your metric and analyses.

Lastly, you have data linking or defining the relationships of the data you have. Always be sure to know the difference between causal and correlational data. Causal is simply a pair of data with one data point affecting another. And correlational data is simply a pair of data with both being affected by an external data.

Chapter 3

Minimum Viable Product: The Root of All Profitable Products

"The MVP has just those features considered sufficient for it to be of value to customers and allow for it to be shipped or sold to early adopters. Customer feedback will inform future development of the product."

—Scott M. Graffius

To obtain that One Metric That Matters, you need to be already data driven. You should have collected the right data. Choose the type of data you wish to use. Figure out their relationships. And then evaluate them.

But to be honest, you don't need to be too intense on finding that metric. You can actually decide upon it for a few seconds. This is especially true if your business is simple.

Once you get to this point, everything will be up to you. Again, the metric depends on the type of business, your goals, and situation. A chosen metric for one business will not work for another.

Anyway, this chapter will talk about minimum viable product. But before that, here are some examples you need to study.

An Example: The Profitable Hotdogs

Saying it like that seems irresponsible and can get you confused and baffled, so here's an example.

Say that your startup is a humble food cart that sells hotdogs. By starting your business lean, it means that you'll man the store yourself. You will also handle everything else. Manage finances, buy the supplies, and market. Also, you will have your single core product: the hotdogs.

You already have a data driven mindset. You care now for statistics and analytics. Together with your cooking equipment, you have a tablet with an inventory and sales app. That app will make it easy for you to track and record data about your stores and customers.

Deciding that the number of hotdogs sold is the One Metric That Matters is a good choice. It's a no-brainer. Your business is too lean and simple for it to need complex analysis. Nonetheless, you still want to gather data for your business just in case.

All you need to do now is operate the business and set your goal. Say that your goal is to make your business handle your daily expenses. You can add the fact that it should also cover at least a percent of the amount you loaned for the business per week.

Thanks to your business setup, you can easily connect with your customers. You can take advantage of connecting with them personally. It's a good opportunity to talk to them while they wait for their food.

Through this, you can easily gather enough information from your customer. You can ask how they like your product. You can also fish for information if there's anything they would want from it that will make them buy more from you. At this rate, forming connections with them will be fast and easy. In return, they can give you tons of feedback.

You've heard what they have to say about your stall, product, and you. Now you know that they would prefer their hotdogs to be sandwiched. You got a new idea, and you have now a new product: hotdog sandwich.

As you go about your business, you then check the efficiency of your operations. You found out that there was no need for you to have an ice box. You used to keep your hotdogs cool inside it to prevent spoilage. Now you don't need it since all your stocks are consumed the same day you bought them.

You then removed that unneeded element and made your stall a bit more efficient. Removing the icebox removed the expense of buying dry ice for it. Also, completely removing it from the business process made it faster to cook the hotdogs. It's faster to cook because they're not ice cold, so you don't need to thaw them.

After the change, you noticed the number of customers increased. It was most probably because of the faster cooking time, which was the result of eliminating the ice box. Your One Metric That Matters is showing you now that your business is getting better.

The next step you did was to apply some improvements. It was an easy thing to think of.

You just need to buy more hotdogs because you always come home without any hotdog. The move is beneficial since you can sell more of your products. It also reduced the number of times you need to visit your supplier.

Since your business is doing well now, it's time for you to check on the data you gathered. What you have primarily is your sales history. The data it contained was easily comparable, understandable, rate-able, and relevant. You have complete control of your business.

You were able to know that you sell very well during the weekends. That's thanks to your sales history. You decided to bring more hotdogs during those days to maximize your sales.

Counter Example: The Demand for Ice Cream

Of course, the previous example seems too good to be true since the customers are just gobbling up the hotdogs. But here's a similar example, but didn't have the same customers. The entrepreneur has used lean startup methodology and lean analytics, too.

The example again is a food cart that sells hotdogs. It's running lean; the only difference is the owner chose a bad location. Low foot traffic, and nobody's really interested in buying hotdogs on the street.

Hotdogs sales is still the One Metric That Matters. The owner of this hotdog stall started operating with the same goal as the previous example.

With a measly number of customers and foot traffic, the owner can't connect to customers well. Nonetheless, he pursued gathering data by interviewing the locals. He was able to know that people in the area don't particularly like hotdogs.

He then asked them what they preferred. They preferred ice cream instead. In this case, the product he built failed in the measurement cycle. In the learn cycle, he learned that he'll get nowhere with hotdogs, but ice cream has a higher chance of getting sold.

Thankfully, he didn't hire anyone. He only bought a simple stall with a propane tank, gas burner, fryer, ice box, and acrylic food display. So, if he wants to convert into an ice cream stall, all he need is to get rid of the tank, burner, and fryer. He needs to replace them with an ice cream canister and an ice cream scooper. He can place the cones and containers on the acrylic display.

He has done that, and he settled for a single flavor: vanilla. After a few days, he sold a decent amount, but the metric is telling him that he's still not doing well. After a week, he realized something. The low foot traffic in his location is really hurting his business.

He now has to decide on two things since even if his product has potential, he can't build a business around it. He could either call it quits; or he could move to a place with more people.

Either way, he can freely decide without stressing himself. The amount of money he has spent on the business was minimal; the losses he incurred was not great.

Application Overview

The examples showed how simple and convenient lean startup and lean analytics is. And there's a high chance you were already doing it before you stumbled upon this book.

Doing things lean made the operation of the startup easier simple and easier. It also removed the fear and stress of failure. It's not that you expect yourself to fail. But with lean, you know that you'll not hit rock-bottom if your first attempt doesn't work out.

And even if doesn't work out, you still have the option to continue or just stop. You have full control. You don't actually fail, but you'll just experience a setback.

On the other hand, you might have noticed that both examples only have one product to sell. That's because both examples are using a minimum viable product or MVP. The term has been thrown in the previous sections a few times. But what is it exactly?

Minimum Viable Product

Most people don't just view lean analytics as a product development cycle. They view it as the best approach with producing a minimum viable product or MVP.

Most lean startups mainly rely on MVPs. They are products that can solve a problem. They can satisfy a need. They don't have the bells and whistles or any secondary features or functions.

An MVP is a product in its simplest form. It can give you profit with minimal effort and resources. Putting it like that, it's fundamentally similar to lean startup. Instead of a lean business, MVPs are lean products.

For example, if you have a food cart or stall, you can treat a simple scrambled egg as your minimum viable product. The ingredients of this scrambled egg are egg, a bit of salt, and cooking oil for frying. Access to the ingredients is a non-issue since they are commercially available anywhere.

Processing the ingredients to make a scrambled egg requires minimal effort and skill. And on its core, it can simply alleviate the hunger of your customer.

You can develop your MVP using the BML (build, measure, and learn) development cycle. This process can make your scrambled egg a more profitable product.

To get started with BML, you need to start with an idea, which is parallel with your goal. Say that your goal is to develop a tasty product or scrambled egg. One of the most viable ideas you can build into your product is to improve your ingredients.

You can start with replacing your cooking oil with butter. Build the idea, and test it out to your customers to start the measuring process. Select the one metric that matters in this phase. You can just use the number of sales you gain or loss as the metric. Record the data you gathered and analyze the data.

If the number of sold scrambled eggs improves, start the cycle again and build the new idea. That idea is the usage of butter. If you experience losses, then you can let go of the butter, and rethink of a new idea. Using sea salt instead of regular fine salt might be a good idea to implement.

The Perfect Product

As you progress and go through countless BML cycles, your MVP becomes a perfect product. A perfected product can help you answer the second core question in your business. Can you build a business around your product?

This perfect product can help you sustain your business. But if the metric goes down, you can just retreat your product for another round of development cycle.

Why MVPs?

An MVP is the simplest form of a product. In most cases, it is designed to lure in early adopters or your first customers. Minimum viable products are like beta versions of a video game. They contain all the features to get beta testers hooked.

For those who are unfamiliar, beta testers are people who test the game. They are given the privilege to be the first ones to play it before it's released to the market. The games are either given free or discounted to beta testers.

In exchange, game developers expect those testers to provide feedback. The feedback is expected to help them fix any issue found in the game. This, in turn raises the game's quality for the market.

Taking advantage of an MVP makes it easier for businesses. Startups in particular tend to use MVPs to find a profitable product they can use now and later in the future.

It is also less costly since they will be getting refined data from reliable sources. These sources are the beta testers. They are reliable since they have a large amount of interest towards the products.

And they don't care if the product is incomplete. They recognize the potential. They are willing to endure any concerns or flaws of the product just to have a shot at it.

They would even shell out money even if it's bare. And they don't care if the only features the provided are the minimum. They also love the fact that they can be considered the pioneers or called the early adopters/beta testers.

MVPs attract getting reliable feedback. It also saves the business from the cost of hiring R&D people or analysts. It also poses minimal risks. The numbers of early adopters are few after all.

Compared to waiting to perfect a product, launching it in full production once assumed it's ready for the market, learning later that it will flop in the market, and receiving tons of complaints from customers, letting a small number of people hate you for an unpolished product is a small price to pay.

The Early Adopters

As you might have already perceived, the early adopters are the key for MVPs to work. Since lean startup and analytics rely on MVPs to succeed, early adopters become immensely crucial if you want your business to succeed.

Due to that, you should prioritize the hunt for early adopters after the first build development cycle.

Also, take note that aside from being reliable sources of feedback, early adopters are also more forgiving compared to regular customers. They also tend to provide more feedback since they are proven to be already interested in the product you give them.

Lastly, taking advantage of them allows you to avoid developing or creating the wrong product for your target customers.

MVPs' Other Purposes

Here are the other purposes of minimum viable products aside from using them to achieve the perfect product with minimal risk and higher success rate:

1. It makes it faster and easier for the businesses to learn about the strengths and weaknesses of a new product.
2. It's easier and faster to test a prototype product with minimal resources used.
3. It prevents wasting time in adding more features and bloating the product.
4. Feedback generated from the MVP can be used on other products.
5. The MVP can also become a base for another product even if it fails.
6. It gauges the skill and power of the product development team or the startup itself. It tests if the actual company and its target goals is viable,

7. Aside from being a good marketing material for early adopters, word of the products and bawdiness' existence can easily get around the neighborhood.

MVP as Prototypes and Visions

Despite using the word minimum, there's no standard when it comes to the actual minimum features or cost to be used on an MVP. It's up to the organization and its resources on what the actual minimum is.

Because of that, it's much easier to refer to MVP as a product prototype. It's easier to understand, and it's much more of a familiar term.

Since MVPs are basically product prototypes, the main test for the product isn't to know the features that should be applied on it. Instead, the test is to know if the product is viable for the business to create and sell.

Despite being regarded as prototypes, you should treat MVPs as products. It's just a vision that you sell to visionaries and not customers. What comes out of it is the actual product you would sell to customers. Most often than not, MVPs are used as marketing materials.

Minimum Viable Service and Collective Minimum Viable Product

For you startup, creating an MVP allows you to focus on one single product that you will rely on. You might have some doubts on how it will work, especially if you have a retail store that serves multiple products and you can't exactly improve the products you are selling. But MVP isn't limited to only products.

You can also apply lean startup and analytics on services. Also, you can treat all of your products into one and call it your MVP. For example, if you want to run a liquor store, you can treat all the liquors you have as one product.

You can do that by collectively treating them as your Minimum Viable Service. Your liquor store will start with the minimum viable products like a single brand of the most popular beer, spirit, and wine.

As you go with your business, you will surely encounter people looking for certain brands and liquor. You can take note of their requests and just stock up on those brands that they mentioned.

Instead of treating a single product as your MVP, you're going to treat your whole stock as a single minimum viable service.

Takeaway

A business running lean would always start with a minimum viable product or service. Instead of selling or providing multiple products or collections of products, you start with the ones with the highest chance of satisfying customers and providing you with profit.

As your business grows and you follow lean analytics, you can turn that minimum viable product as the perfect product. Thanks to the build, measure, and learn cycle, your product can progress into something more profitable, which would then also help your business improve.

You should also remember that aside from running lean and minimizing risks, your MVP can serve other purposes.

On another note, you must also make sure that you have early adopters. These people are the ones that will help you jumpstart your business and assist you in attaining your perfect product or service.

And when you deal with your MVP and early adopters, always remind yourself that your MVP is not a product, but a vision you're selling to them. It only becomes a product if your early adopters accept it as such.

Now that you have a full idea on the importance and positive effects of minimum viable products, lean startup, lean analysis, and a data-driven mindset to your business, the next step is to know what their disadvantages are, the oppositions' opinions about them, and how to circumvent those disadvantages and flaws.

Chapter 4

The Opposition and Words of the Wise

"Perfectionism is a disease. Procrastination is a disease. ACTION is the cure."

—Richie Norton

There is one big flaw in lean startup and analytics. It is the tendency to put all the work into the entrepreneur. It's true that the methodology and approach reduces a lot of the required resources to run a business. However, in turn, the entrepreneur needs to work twice as much.

On the other hand, proponents defend that going lean isn't about the money. It isn't about preventing quality of life improvements in the business. It's not about not hiring employees. They say that running lean means working with customers solely. It's designed to work like that, instead of pushing efforts on different directions.

Detractors also mention about the methodology being too product centric. They argue that having the best product shouldn't be the only goal of a business.

Simplifying a business to the point that it only revolves around its product can be a huge pitfall. A business isn't all about making and selling. There are other faces an entrepreneur must consider when operating. A few of them are marketing, logistics, accounting, and even legal.

Nonetheless, you could have already identified that the methodology has addressed this issue. Most of the points from the opposition have been already addressed.

Against Minimum Viable Product

Minimum Viable Product has been split into multiple types. This is to avoid the tendency of a business to rely and focus too much on one product. Second, proponents have already gone preaching to make metric flexible. It's supposed to be dynamic, according to the ever-changing needs of their businesses.

However, followers of lean analytics should know that MVP is not always the solution. It is not the only way to grow your business. This is especially true if you're in the latter stages of your business' life. Producing or releasing a lackluster product can be detrimental. An MVP with your recognizable business name on it can backfire on you.

More established businesses have been adopting lean startup methodologies. And they're not doing any good to the entrepreneurship community. MVP should be reserved to startups. There are other forms of products like MVP, but are well suited to bigger companies.

Also, even if you're a startup, you can actually get away from using MVP and its risks. The key is to use the MVP of your competitors. Yes, that sounds awful, but that's business.

Don't risk your name by releasing a product on its weakest state. You can actually get the data you need without an MVP. That method is to check out your competition's MVPs.

Google and Facebook didn't slowly climb their way up to success by pioneering a product line from an

MVP. They skipped the build and measure cycles, and started on the learn cycle first.

The competitors they had were AOL/Yahoo and Multiply/Friendster respectively. The two companies did the measure and build cycles for their competitors' MVPs. They didn't battle directly with MVP vs. MVP. They immediately created better and robust versions of their competitors' products.

Against the Metric

Another point that the opposition makes is the one metric that matters. It's true that it's nice to only check one metric alone to gauge the current condition of a company. However, it's a pipe dream. A business, especially as it grows, is a complex mechanism.

You just can't measure it with one metric alone. You can't synthesize metrics into one single metric that can tell you everything. A business is dynamic. Its needs change every time. One metric will not be able to provide such accurate insight on the current state of a business.

Some people and experts believe that an MVP can actually provide more harm than benefits to a company or a startup. AN MVP creates a risk. That risk is when a competitor decides to copy the MVP and get a head start on developing the actual product.

Also, it can be said that the negative feedback can hurt the company. Plus, early adopters who have no idea about the concept of MVP can become detractors.

They may think that the almost featureless product is the actual product. And they would rather find another which is already completed and feature rich.

Most entrepreneurs believe that the metric should be complex. But it should be also simplified, effective, but creative. No. It doesn't have to be like that. And those characteristics are too oxymoronic.

The metric should be a measure of your progress. It shouldn't be creative or flashy. You should focus on functionality over form. If the number of sales gives you an idea if you're doing well, then use it. Don't create calculations or synthesize a lot of data points just to say you have the perfect metric. That's not the point of your business.

How to Avoid Making Mistakes with Lean Analytics

Entrepreneurs are everywhere and one too many. Don't be lax just because you're running lean. Never forget that doing lean startup and analytics isn't a surefire method to be successful. The two are a methodology and approach in business. They help a startup stand their ground despite the lack of financial power.

You should avoid copying how today's billionaires become successful. You don't need to drop out from college or to start your company in a garage. Don't be a pseudo-visionary. Don't lead your business with weird and unheard-of business tactics.

Always remind yourself that entrepreneurship is mostly about management. Changes and innovations don't happen frequently in the industry. This is the truth regardless of trends and dynamisms. Before you try something new, be sure that you already have a solid foundation.

Also, don't ever think that a business is just about its products and selling it. It's true that lean startup preaches about focusing on products and customers. However, it doesn't mean that you can forget about the other technicalities of running a business.

Startups are not just about developing creating, and selling the perfect product. A startup is also created to identify or discover if a certain line of business is viable. It also tests if the entrepreneur does really have what it takes to run a business. That's why lean startup and analysis is heavily favored by the modern entrepreneur.

In addition, a startup business is an organization that you need to manage in order to be successful. Many techniques and methodologies have been developed. These techniques allow beginners to manage their startups in a more effective way. Be sure not to only learn about lean. You should also know about other methodologies and approaches in business.

Never skip the boring stuff. As an entrepreneur, you should always be accountable. You should learn how to measure your progress and successes. You should know how to make goals. You also need to know where and what you need to prioritize.

Lastly, it always boils down to: build or turn ideas to products. Measure how your customers respond to your ideas or products. Learn if you can continue creating and selling the product or if you need to stop and develop a new one.

Regardless of methodologies, the simple build, measure, and learn development cycle is present. Even if you don't like lean startup or analytics, you shouldn't disregard this form of development cycle.

Takeaway

The key takeaway here is that lean startup and analytics are not perfect. They have flaws, and they can't be treated as a meal ticket to success. And for you to take full advantage of it, you must embrace some of its flaws.

Firstly, expect that it would be difficult. Running a lean business is simple, but it's taxing. You're sacrificing many conveniences to run. Use as little resources as you can, but don't expect profit large enough to sustain the business.

Second, center around your business on your product and customers. Remember that if those two fail or disappear, you're already a goner. If the inflow of your customers grinds to a halt, immediately focus on getting them back. The same with your product. If your product isn't selling, improve that product or replace it with something much better.

Third, minimum viable product is controversial. It sounds good on paper, but it can bring in some problems. This is especially true if you keep on using one even at the latter stages of your business life.

Remember that MVP is effective during the early stages of your business. As much as possible, you should only have one. When you have perfected your product, you should change your business methods and practices.

Fourth, never forget that your metric changes together with your current business goals. It can't be stressed enough. Be sure to be always aware with the data you gather for your metric, too.

Just to remind you, the metric is good and all. What always goes wrong with it is how entrepreneurs use it and interpret its importance.

Fifth, you can follow everything in this book, but you can still make mistakes. Lean startups and analytics don't save entrepreneurs if they make a mess. They're only guides and roadmaps to make your startup survive. The early stages of a business are tough. You need to follow the guide to make it easier for your emotional and cognitive health. Starting a business without any concrete idea on what you need to do or what's going on can make you crazy, you know.

Lastly, you're already at the end of this book. Congratulations in advance. What's left for you to do now is check out the last part, which will nicely wrap everything up. If you can, it might be good for you to have a good review of the previous chapters. Just to be sure that you got everything right.

Conclusion

Here's a curve ball for you: data is the oil of the 21st century. It is what makes people billionaires. The era of coal mining and software development to enrich oneself is over. Acquiring, processing, and analyzing data is the most profitable business now.

Just look at Amazon, Facebook, and Google. The biggest element in their businesses that they have in common is data acquisition. Every day, their businesses harvest information online.

Aside from gaining financial success, data can be used for political power. Just think about the recent election shenanigans. People believe that companies that have control over data have the capability to influence the country's democracy.

A good example of the usage of data for political power is the Cambridge Analytica case. People allege that they have harvested personal information from voters through Facebook.

They processed the data they gathered, and then developed an AI that can predict a person's future

75

decisions. It sounds like a story ripped from a science fiction book, but it's real. And you can observe it. Just log in to your Facebook account.

Try messaging a friend and mention a brand or product in your chat. Close the chat box, and refresh your timeline. Look at the advertisement on the side of the page. There's a 90% chance that you'll see the product or brand you mentioned on the ad that's placed there.

That's how powerful data is. There's no reason you shouldn't take advantage of its power. You can do that with apps and tools that are overly available to everyone.

Lean analytics is an approach that has become a "must do" for every startup ever since it was conceived. It will be difficult for any entrepreneur to work half ass. It is important to establish lean startup without lean analytics.

Success is now measurable by just flicking your fingers on a smartphone. Progress can be easily monitored by reviewing a digital spreadsheet on your laptop. And data can be gathered by a static website you made months before. You can gather data with it without you speaking any words to any customer.

Technology has made starting a business as easy as playing a computer game. However, it doesn't change the fact that you'll still need real money to start a business. And it's the biggest hindrance of them all when you're new.

Nonetheless, by playing it a bit safe, focusing on the most important parts of the business, minimizing risks, and using data to help you with your decisions, you'll be able to hold your ground and achieve success.

Anyway, just to close this book off on a high note, here's a quick rundown of what you need to do to get started with lean startup and analytics.

Create a goal for your business. It's the first step after you start your operations.

Second, pick the metric that you want to use to measure the progress of your business towards the goal you set. Don't overcomplicate it. Just make sure that it can really measure your progress.

Third, create plans on how you can improve the numbers of your metric. Test the plans out and see which is the most effective. Measure the effectiveness of the plans or actions.

Fourth, choose the most effective method. Discard or save the rest for later. Exhaust the most effective plan you have. Once it doesn't bring you towards your goal, reevaluate if the current business goal is still relevant.

Lastly, repeat the whole process all over again.

Do the same with your product. It doesn't matter if you call it your prototype, first product, or minimum viable product. The goal here is process its improvements through lean analytics. The main goal is to improve it until you can build a stable business around it.

As a follow up, always remember the five major benefits of lean startup and analytics.

1. Decisions are heavily based on data instead of an executive's gut feeling.
2. Development of products and services is faster.
3. Improvements done to existing products and services are faster. Products and services are flexible and will always change for the better.

4. High quality feedback from stakeholders and consumers is easily attainable.

5. Improved customer perception and company reputation.

Going back to what I promised, the discussions and examples in this book demonstrate the huge potential of lean startup and analytics in your business.

It's true that more workload is coming your way if you follow the steps indicated in this book. However, the reward on doing the steps is that you can go about your business knowing what direction you are going.

I've been like you. In my first business, I was so lost on what's going on. I questioned myself everyday if I can get through every month with my business. In the end, I didn't. Because I had no idea on what the hell was going on with my startup.

But, unlike me, you have the proper knowledge on how to get through that. If you want to avoid getting stuck with a business loan for a business that already failed, then just follow the advice listed here.

The steps make sense for those who have limited resources or for those who just want to have a solid foundation for their business without the huge risks.

Unlike traditional methods on building business, lean startup and analytics let you start faster with minimal restrictions on your budget. In exchange, you will have a relatively small business that functions as if it's a medium sized one.

And at this point, I believe every word you need to hear or read has been laid out. This book will be always at your disposal any time you need to refresh what you have learned today. I wish you well and good luck to you and your business.

Thank you

Before you go, I just wanted to say thank you for purchasing my book.

You could have picked from dozens of other books on the same topic but you took a chance and chose this one.

So, a HUGE thanks to you for getting this book and for reading all the way to the end.

Now I wanted to ask you for a small favor. ***Could you please consider posting a review on the platform? Reviews are one of the easiest ways to support the work of independent authors.***

This feedback will help me continue to write the type of books that will help you get the results you want. So if you enjoyed it, please let me know.

References

Alistair Croll, B. Y. (n.d.). *Use data to build a better startup faster*. Retrieved from Lean Anaylitcs Book: http://leananalyticsbook.com

Brekel, B. (2017, April 11). *Why Lean Startup Doesn't Always Work in Corporates as it Does in Startups*. Retrieved from Revel X: https://www.revelx.co/blog/why-lean-startup-doesnt-always-work-in-corporates/

Burgstone, J. (n.d.). *What's Wrong With the Lean Start-up*. Retrieved from Inc.: https://www.inc.com/jon-burgstone/flaws-in-the-lean-start-up.html

DeMeré, N. E. (2016, July 8). *Lean Analytics: Why the "One Metric" is more complicated than it sounds ft. Notion Data* . Retrieved from Use Notion: https://blog.usenotion.com/lean-analytics-why-the-one-metric-is-more-complicated-than-it-sounds-7ba02d2aa718

DigitalPrinciples. (n.d.). *Be Data Driven*. Retrieved from Principles for Digital Development: https://digitalprinciples.org/principle/be-data-driven/

Innov8rs. (2018, February 12). *Let's Get Real: Why Lean Startup Is NOT Right For Everyone*. Retrieved from Innov8rs: https://innov8rs.co/news/lets-get-real-lean-startup-not-right-everyone/

Jongen, R. (2018, November 6). *What Is Lean Analytics, and How Do You Apply It*. Retrieved from Revel X: https://www.revelx.co/blog/what-is-lean-analytics/

Lownie, K. (2013, October 7). *Minimum Viable Service: Why Less is Best When it Comes to SaaS Customer Service*. Retrieved from Open View Partners: https://openviewpartners.com/blog/minimum-viable-service-less-best/

Patel, N. (n.d.). *Neil Patel*. Retrieved from Using Lean Analytics Principles to Build a Strong Company: https://neilpatel.com/blog/lean-analytics/

Reies, E. (2011, June 14). *Open Innovation in DC*. Retrieved from Startup Lessons Learned: http://www.startuplessonslearned.com/2011/06/open-innovation-in-dc.html

Reis, E. (n.d.). *Principles*. Retrieved from The Lean Startup Methodology: http://theleanstartup.com/principles

RevelX. (2017, March 10). *Medium*. Retrieved from Why Lean Startup Doesn't Always Work in Corporates as it Does in

Startups:
https://medium.com/@RevelX/why-lean-startup-doesnt-always-work-in-corporates-as-it-does-in-startups-35a6a3c7f606

Sanon, M. (2017, April 28). *4 Reasons Why Data Analytics is Important.* Retrieved from Digital Vidya: https://www.digitalvidya.com/blog/reasons-data-analytics-important/

www.ingramcontent.com/pod-product-compliance
Lightning Source LLC
Chambersburg PA
CBHW071440210326

41597CB00020B/3886